M000080890

The
Curmudgeon
Woman

The Curmudgeon Woman

Compiled and edited by
Nancy M. Henley and
Jacqueline D. Goodchilds

Andrews McMeel
Publishing

Kansas City

The Curmudgeon Woman

copyright © 2000 by Nancy M. Henley and Jacqueline D. Goodchilds. All rights reserved.
Printed in the United States of America. No part of this book may be used or reproduced
in any manner whatsoever without written permission except in the case of reprints
in the context of reviews. For information, write Andrews McMeel Publishing,
an Andrews McMeel Universal company, 4520 Main Street, Kansas City, Missouri 64111.

00 01 02 03 04 BIN 10 9 8 7 6 5 4 3 2 1

Library of Congress Cataloging-in-Publication Data
The curmudgeon woman / compiled and edited by Nancy M. Henley and Jacqueline D.
Goodchilds.
     p. cm.
  ISBN 0-7407-1007-9 (pbk.)
     1. Women—Quotations. 2. Quotations, English. I. Henley, Nancy. II. Goodchilds,
Jacqueline D. (Jacqueline Desire), 1926–

PN6081.5 .C87 2000
305.4—dc21   00-030478

Book design by Holly Camerlinck

─────────── **Attention: Schools and Businesses** ───────────

Andrews McMeel books are available at quantity discounts with bulk purchase for
educational, business, or sales promotional use. For information, please write to:
Special Sales Department, Andrews McMeel Publishing, 4520 Main Street,
Kansas City, Missouri 64111.

Contents

Foreword

The concept of *curmudgeon woman* may be new to many people, may seem indeed like a contradiction in terms. Isn't a *curmudgeon* male, old, and cranky? There are plenty of terms for old, cranky women—*crone, hag, harridan,* and *harpy* come to mind. Can a woman be a curmudgeon? What exactly is a curmudgeon, anyway?

The roots of the word are unknown; the *Oxford English Dictionary* (2nd ed., on-line) finds a first printed reference in 1577. *Curmudgeon* once meant "miser," but it has lost that archaic meaning for the more modern one given in dictionaries of a "crusty," "irascible," "ill-tempered," "often old," "usually old," "often elderly" person or man.

When we asked eight knowledgeable friends and colleagues their interpretations of the word *curmudgeon,* all but one used some term referring to a negative disposition or personality trait: *cantankerous, crotchety, crusty, grouchy, gruff, grumpy* (they're sounding like the seven dwarfs), *mean, negativist, obstreperous, recalcitrant.* Five of them described a curmudgeon as an older person, and four described the curmudgeon only as male.

Jon Winokur, who has collected curmudgeonly sayings in his various wickedly enjoyable books, gives a modern definition for curmudgeon that captures our understanding of the term as well:

anyone who hates hypocrisy and pretense and has the temerity to say so; anyone with the habit of pointing out unpleasant facts in an engaging and humorous manner.[1]

Winokur includes quotations from women in his books; in fact he names twenty women—such as Tallulah Bankhead, Molly Ivins,

[1] Jon Winokur, *The Portable Curmudgeon* (New York: New American Library, 1987), p. iii.

and Dorothy Parker—as "world-class curmudgeons."[2] Yet women make up only 13 percent of that list.

To remedy this situation of the invisible woman curmudgeon, we have gathered five hundred superbly biting and witty quotations by over three hundred women we consider curmudgeonly. The topics range from God's nature to the devil's, from sex to artistic creativity, but these women seem especially concerned with women's lot, with men, and with women's relation to men. This seems only logical: Curmudgeons are given to complaining, and women certainly have a complaint with their position relative to men's in the world. All the quotations meet our idea of what makes a remark curmudgeonly: It has wit; it is negative, that is, against received wisdom; and it states some deeper truth.

It wasn't easy selecting these quotations; from the thousands that we considered, we culled over 850. Then by successive

---

[2] Jon Winokur, *The Portable Curmudgeon Redux* (New York: Dutton, 1992), pp. 4–6.

scrutinies we trimmed them to what we consider the best five hundred, representing the sweep of curmudgeon-woman thought over the centuries, which we present herein. We make no assumption that we have covered the universe of curmudgeon-woman quotations, although eventually we were encountering the same quotations in many different sources, one sign that we had found the major examples. We don't pretend these will be everyone's favorites, either; one of yours might be missing.

We found the whole experience of searching for curmudgeon women one of the most pleasing, funny, uplifting, and gratifying of our lives. We hope that being in the company of these great contrarian thinkers and wits will thrill our readers as it did us. We also hope that if there are closeted curmudgeon women out there, this book will encourage them to come out of their closets and share their nasty insights with the rest of the world.

About this book:

The quotations of *Curmudgeon Woman* are organized in fifteen broad categories, each of which constitutes a chapter of this book. Within these categories, quotations are arranged alphabetically by author. In addition, there is an author index at the back of the book, in which the reader may find individual authors, with the dates that place them in their historical periods.

Observations

at Large

Experience is a good teacher, but
she sends in terrific bills.

—**Minna Antrim**

Fortune, in its workings,
has something in common with the slot-machine.
There are those who can bait it forever
and never get more than
an odd assortment of lemons for their pains.

—**Dorothy Baker**

YOU COME INTO THE WORLD ALONE

and you go out of the world alone,

yet it seems to me

you are more alone while living

than even going and coming.

—**Emily Carr**

There are only two
or three human stories,
and they go on
repeating themselves
as fiercely as if
they had never
happened before.

—**Willa Cather**

All people are made alike.
They are made of bone, flesh
  and dinners.
Only the dinners are different.

—Gertrude Louise Cheney

I distrusted work, disliked it.
I thought it was a very bad thing that the
human race had unfortunately
invented for itself.

—**Agatha Christie**

———————

Happiness is too many things these days
for anyone to wish it on anyone lightly.
So let's just wish each other a bileless
New Year and leave it at that.

—**Judith Crist**

No one is so keen to gather
ever newer impressions as those
who do not know how to process
the old ones.

—**Marie von Ebner-Eschenbach**

We are so vain that we value the opinion
even of those whose opinions
we find worthless.

—**Marie von Ebner-Eschenbach**

Prophecy is the most gratuitous form of error.

—George Eliot

Instant gratification takes too long.

—Carrie Fisher

THERE WAS A TIME WHEN PATIENCE

ceased to be a virtue.

It was long ago.

—**Charlotte Perkins Gilman**

Life is not orderly.
No matter how we try
to make life so,
right in the middle of it
we die,
lose a leg,
fall in love,
drop a jar of apple sauce.

—Natalie Goldberg

Living in a vacuum sucks.

—Adrienne E. Gusoff

Not only is life a bitch, it has puppies.

—Adrienne E. Gusoff

The Goddamn human race deserves itself, and as far as I'm concerned it can have it.

—Elizabeth Janeway

*S*OME MINDS REMAIN OPEN

long enough

for the truth not only to enter

but to pass on through

by way of a ready exit

without pausing anywhere

along the route.

—Sister Elizabeth Kenny

"Hope is the feeling you have
that the feeling you have isn't permanent."

—Jean Kerr

You can fool all of the people
some of the time, and some of the people
all of the time. And that's sufficient.

—Rose King

This life isn't bad for a first draft.

—Joan Konner

LIFE IS SOMETHING TO DO

when you can't get to sleep.

—**Fran Lebowitz**

ORIGINAL THOUGHT IS LIKE ORIGINAL SIN:

both happened before you were born

to people you could not possibly have met.

—**Fran Lebowitz**

When action grows unprofitable,
gather information;
when information grows unprofitable,
sleep.

—**Ursula K. Le Guin**

I have a simple philosophy.
Fill what's empty. Empty what's full.
And scratch where it itches.

—**Alice Roosevelt Longworth**

No good deed goes unpunished.

—Clare Boothe Luce

Readers are plentiful: thinkers are rare.

—**Harriet Martineau**

It's not true that life is
one damn thing after another—
it's one damn thing over and over.

—**Edna St. Vincent Millay**

Life goes on forever
like the gnawing of a mouse.

—**Edna St. Vincent Millay**

Snags alone are not so dangerous—
it's the debris that clings to them
that makes the trouble.

—Anne Shannon Monroe

When a creature is witty enough,
he will occasionally say something
that smacks of the profound.

—Rose O'Neill

Parables are unnecessary
for recognizing the blatant absurdity
of everyday life.
Reality is lesson enough.

—Jane O'Reilly

A cruel story runs on wheels,
and every hand oils the wheels
as they run.

—Ouida

EVERY YEAR, BACK SPRING COMES,

with nasty little birds,

yapping their fool heads off,

and the ground all mucked up

with arbutus.

—**Dorothy Parker**

People who cannot recognize
a palpable absurdity are very much
in the way of civilization.

—Agnes Repplier

Science may carry us to Mars,
but it will leave the earth peopled as ever
by the inept.

—Agnes Repplier

Next week, or next month, or next year I'll kill myself. But I might as well last out my month's rent, which has been paid up, and my credit for breakfast in the morning.

—Jean Rhys

I have come to the conclusion, after many years of sometimes sad experience, that you cannot come to any conclusion at all.

—Vita Sackville-West

Sanity is a cozy lie.

—Susan Sontag

I suspect anyone self-satisfied
enough to refuse lawful pleasure:
we are not sufficiently rich
in our separate resources to reject
the graces of the universe
when offered.

—Freya Stark

Never face facts; if you do
you'll never get up in the morning.

—**Marlo Thomas**

She quoted a friend
who used to say
any advice is good
as long as it is strong enough.

—**Alice B. Toklas**

WHAT IS SAUCE FOR THE GOOSE

may be sauce for the gander,

but is not necessarily sauce for the chicken,

the duck, the turkey, or the guinea hen.

—Alice B. Toklas

"I personally think we developed language
because of our deep inner need
to complain."

—Jane Wagner

"Just remember, we're all in this alone."

—Jane Wagner

"Reality is the leading cause of stress
for those in touch with it."

—Jane Wagner

Life is not an easy thing to embrace,
like trying to hug an elephant.

—Diane Wakoski

Too much of a good thing
can be wonderful.

—Mae West

Mental health, like dandruff,
crops up when you least expect it.

—Robin Worthington

The Importance of Appearance

I do not say that I was ever
what I would call "plain,"
but I have the sort of face that bores me
when I see it on other people.

—**Margot Asquith**

To a woman, the consciousness of being
well-dressed gives a sense of tranquillity
which religion fails to bestow.

—**Helen Olcott Bell**

I NEVER GO OUT UNLESS I LOOK LIKE

Joan Crawford the movie star.

If you want to see the girl next door,

go next door.

—Joan Crawford

A lady is one who never
shows her underwear unintentionally.

—Lillian Day

When a man gets up to speak,
people listen, then look.
When a woman gets up, people *look;*
then, if they like what they see,
they listen.

—Pauline Frederick

Plain women know more about men than beautiful ones do.

—Katharine Hepburn

"Love can't last around poverty. Neither can a woman's looks."

—Kristin Hunter

A good many women are
good tempered simply because
it saves the wrinkles coming too soon.

—Bettina von Hutten

I'm tired of all this nonsense about
beauty being only skin-deep.
That's deep enough. What do you want—
an adorable pancreas?

—Jean Kerr

Any girl can be glamorous.
All you have to do is stand still
and look stupid.

—Hedy Lamarr

Violet will be a good color for hair
at just about the same time
that brunette becomes
a good color for flowers.

—Fran Lebowitz

She always believed in
the old adage "Leave them
while you're looking good."

—**Anita Loos**

All elegant women have acquired
a technique of weeping
which has no . . . fatal effect
on the makeup.

—**Anaïs Nin**

Lots of women buy just as many
wigs and makeup things as I do.
They just don't wear them all
at the same time.

—Dolly Parton

You'd be surprised how much it costs
to look this cheap.

—Dolly Parton

Sexuality

On the contraceptive sponge:

Just a way of making sex seem more like doing the dishes.

—Elayne Boosler

The act of sex, gratifying as it may be, is God's joke on humanity.

—Bette Davis

A woman can look both moral
and exciting—if she also
looks as if it was quite a struggle.

—Edna Ferber

Personally I know nothing about sex
because I've always been married.

—Zsa Zsa Gabor

MY MOTHER SAID IT WAS SIMPLE

to keep a man:

You must be a maid in the living room,

a cook in the kitchen,

and a whore in the bedroom.

I said I'd hire the other two

and take care of the bedroom bit.

—Jerry Hall

Love, I find, is like singing.
Everybody can do enough
to satisfy themselves,
though it may not impress
the neighbors as being very much.

—Zora Neale Hurston

Response to a male heckler's query "Are you a lesbian?":

Are you my alternative?

—Florynce Kennedy

The witty woman especially
is a tragic figure in America.
Wit destroys eroticism and
eroticism destroys wit, so a woman
must choose between taking lovers
and taking no prisoners.

—Florence King

Women complain about sex
more often than men.
Their gripes fall into two major categories:
(1) Not enough. (2) Too much.

—Ann Landers

I did not sleep. I never do when I am
over-happy, over-unhappy, or in bed
with a strange man.

—Edna O'Brien

Reporting on a Yale prom:

If all those sweet young
things present
were laid end to end,
I wouldn't be at all surprised.

—**Dorothy Parker**

A man may talk inspiringly about love in the abstract—but the look in his eyes is always perfectly concrete.

—Helen Rowland

No man can understand why a woman should prefer a good reputation to a good time.

—Helen Rowland

Mrs. Margaret Sanger said
the best birth control
is to make your husband sleep on the roof.

—Adela Rogers St. Johns

Continence is a habit more compelling
than tomcatting. Enough tomcatting
sooner or later acts as its own cure.
Continence does not cure continence.
There are more reformed rakes than
reformed celibates.

—Jessamyn West

It's hard to be funny
when you have to be clean.

—Mae West

She's the kind of girl who climbed the
ladder of success, wrong by wrong.

—Mae West

When women go wrong,
men go right after them.

— Mae West

*S*EX IS THE TABASCO SAUCE

which an adolescent national palate

sprinkles on every course in the menu.

—Mary Day Winn

I rely on my personality
for birth control.

—Liz Winston

W hat you think is the heart
may well be another organ.

—Jeanette Winterson

Relationships
(Men and Women)

In real love you want the other person's good.
In romantic love you want the other person.

—Margaret Anderson

I married beneath me—all women do.

—Nancy Astor

Marriage. The beginning and the end
are wonderful. But the middle part is hell.

—Enid Bagnold

MARRIAGE ALWAYS DEMANDS

the greatest understanding

of the art of insincerity possible

between two human beings.

—Vicki Baum

Wedlock—the deep, deep peace
of the double bed after the hurly-burly
of the chaise-longue.

—Beatrice (Mrs. Patrick) Campbell

The very fact that we make
such a to-do over golden weddings
indicates our amazement at human endurance.
The celebration is more in the nature of
a reward for stamina.

—Ilka Chase

The trouble with some women
is that they get all
excited about nothing—
and then marry him.

—Cher

We don't elope nowadays,
   and we don't divorce,
   except out of kindness.

— Jenny Churchill

Give me a dozen such heart-breaks,
   if that would help me
   to lose a couple of pounds.

—Colette

I never married because there was no need. I have three pets at home which answer the same purpose as a husband. I have a dog which growls every morning, a parrot which swears all afternoon, and a cat that comes home late at night.

—Marie Corelli

Women are doormats and have been,
The years these mats applaud—
They keep the men from going in
With muddy feet to God.

—**Mary Carolyn Davies**

Marriage is a lottery
in which men stake their liberty
and women their happiness.

—**Virginie des Rieux**

Never go to bed mad.
Stay up and fight.

—**Phyllis Diller**

Any intelligent woman
who reads the marriage contract,
and then goes into it,
deserves all the consequences.

—**Isadora Duncan**

One believes in
rheumatism and true love
only when afflicted by them.

—**Marie von Ebner-Eschenbach**

Being an old maid
is like death by drowning,
a really delightful sensation
after you cease to struggle.

—**Edna Ferber**

I am a marvelous housekeeper.
Every time I leave a man I keep his house.

—Zsa Zsa Gabor

When I'm alone, I can sleep crossways in bed
without an argument.

—Zsa Zsa Gabor

I CAN'T SEE WHY HAVING AN AFFAIR

with someone on and off

is any worse than being married

for a course or two at mealtimes.

—Penelope Gilliatt

In our family we don't divorce
our men—we bury them.

—**Ruth Gordon**

I love being single.
It's almost like being rich.

—**Sue Grafton**

Marriage, for a woman at least,
hampers the two things
that made life to me glorious—
friendship and learning.

—**Jane Harrison**

It is no longer obligatory upon a woman
to give herself to one man
to save herself
from being torn to pieces by the rest.

—**Jennie June**

"Being divorced is like being hit
by a Mack truck. If you live through it,
you start looking very carefully
to the right and to the left."

—Jean Kerr

Marrying a man is like buying something
you've been admiring for a long time
in a shop window. You may love it
when you get it home, but it doesn't always
go with everything else in the house.

—Jean Kerr

LOVE IS MORAL EVEN WITHOUT

legal marriage,

but marriage is immoral

without love.

—**Ellen Key**

The poor wish to be rich,
the rich wish to be happy,
the single wish to be married,
and the married wish to be dead.

—Ann Landers

Not all women give most of their
waking thoughts to the problem
of pleasing men. Some are married.

—**Emma Lee**

Always remember . . . it's
matrimonial suicide to be jealous
when you have a really good reason.

—**Clare Boothe Luce**

Love is like playing checkers.
You have to know which man
to move.

—Jackie "Moms" Mabley

It's like magic. When you
live by yourself, all your
annoying habits are gone!

—Merrill Markoe

72

ANY ONE MUST SEE AT A GLANCE

that if men and women

marry those whom they do not love,

they must love those

whom they do not marry.

—**Harriet Martineau**

"Vinegar he poured on me all his life;
I am well marinated;
how can I be honey now?"

—Tillie Olsen

And in these eyes the love-light lies
And lies—and lies and lies!

—Anita Owen

Behind every successful man
is a surprised woman.

—**Maryon Pearson**

———————

A husband is what is left of the lover
after the nerve has been extracted.

—**Helen Rowland**

A man always mistakes
a woman's clinging devotion for weakness,
until he discovers that it requires
the strength of Samson, the patience of Job,
and the finesse of Solomon to untwine it.

—Helen Rowland

After a few years of marriage
a man can look right at a woman
without seeing her
and a woman can see right through a man
without looking at him.

—Helen Rowland

Before marriage
a man will lie awake
all night thinking
about something you said;
after marriage
he will fall asleep
before you have finished
saying it.

—Helen Rowland

Honeymoons
are the beginning of wisdom—
but the beginning of wisdom
is the end of romance.

—Helen Rowland

In olden times
sacrifices were made at the altar—
a practice which is still continued.

—Helen Rowland

It is easier to keep
half-a-dozen lovers guessing
than to keep one lover
after he has stopped guessing.

—**Helen Rowland**

Love, the quest;
marriage, the conquest;
divorce, the inquest.

—**Helen Rowland**

Marriage
is the only thing
that affords a woman
the pleasure of company
and the perfect sensation
of solitude
at the same time.

—Helen Rowland

One man's folly
is another man's wife.

—Helen Rowland

The honeymoon
is not actually over
until we cease to stifle our sighs
and begin to stifle our yawns.

—Helen Rowland

When a girl marries
she exchanges the attention
of many men
for the inattention of one.

—Helen Rowland

When you see
what some girls marry,
you realize how they must hate
to work for a living.

—Helen Rowland

WHENEVER I DATE A GUY,

I think,

is this the man

I want my children

to spend their weekends with?

—Rita Rudner

I think every woman is entitled
to a middle husband she can forget.

—Adela Rogers St. Johns

It's hard to be growing up in this climate
where sex at its most crude and cold is O.K.
but feeling is somehow indecent.

—May Sarton

ONE OF THE ADVANTAGES

of living alone

is that you don't have to wake up

in the arms of a loved one.

—**Anna Marion Smith**

There you are you see,
quite simple, if you
cannot have your dear husband
for a comfort and a delight,
for a breadwinner
and a crosspatch, for a sofa,
chair or a hot-water bottle,
one can use him as
a cross to be borne.

—**Stevie Smith**

The surest way to be alone
is to get married.

—Gloria Steinem

What a holler would ensue
if people had to pay the minister
as much to marry them as they have to pay
a lawyer to get them a divorce.

—Claire Trevor

Sometimes it is less hard
to wake up feeling lonely
when you are alone
than wake up feeling lonely
when you are with someone.

—Liv Ullmann

Love is much nicer to be in
than an automobile accident,
a tight girdle, a higher tax bracket
or a holding pattern over Philadelphia.

—Judith Viorst

It's all right for a perfect stranger
to kiss your hand
as long as he's perfect.

—Mae West

If our divorce laws were improved,
we could at least say that
if marriage does nobody much good
it does nobody any harm.

—Rebecca West

I think,
therefore I'm single.

—Liz Winston

It was so cold I almost got married.

—Shelley Winters

Parents and Children

Children's talent to endure
stems from their ignorance
of alternatives.

—Maya Angelou

The most effective
form of birth control I know
is spending the day with my kids.

—Jill Bensley

A happy childhood
can't be cured.
Mine'll hang around my neck
like a rainbow,
that's all,
instead of a noose.

—Hortense Calisher

Why do grandparents
and grandchildren
get along so well?
They have the same enemy—
the mother.

—Claudette Colbert

It is not a bad thing
that children should occasionally,
and politely,
put parents in their place.

—Colette

95

Cleaning your house
while your kids are still growing
is like shoveling the walk
before it stops snowing.

—**Phyllis Diller**

As a mother I have served
longer than I expected.

—**Carol Emshwiller**

You may observe mother instinct
at its height in a fond hen
sitting on china eggs—
instinct, but no brains.

—Charlotte Perkins Gilman

The only thing that seems
eternal and natural in motherhood
is ambivalence.

—Jane Lazarre

"Death and taxes and childbirth!
There's never any convenient time
for any of them!"

—**Margaret Mitchell**

I love children,
especially when they cry,
for then someone takes them away.

—**Nancy Mitford**

If you have children,
you never have anything else.

—Kathleen Norris

My husband and I
are either going to buy a dog
or have a child. We can't decide
whether to ruin our carpet
or ruin our lives.

—Rita Rudner

THERE'S A TIME WHEN YOU HAVE TO

explain to your children

why they're born,

and it's a marvelous thing

if you know the reason by then.

—Hazel Scott

Parents can never do too much
for their children to repay them
for the injustice of having
brought them into the world.

—Elizabeth Cady Stanton

The three M's:
Marriage, Motherhood,
and Monotony.

—Evelyn Tension

Americans, indeed,
often seem to be
so overwhelmed
by their children
that they'll do
anything for them
except stay married
to the coproducer.

—Katharine Whitehorn

Aspects of Aging

When I was young I was frightened
I might bore other people, now I'm old
I am frightened they will bore me.

—Ruth Adam

When I was forty, I used to wonder
what people thought of me. Now I wonder
what *I* think of them.

—Brooke Astor

Human nature
is so well disposed
towards those
in interesting situations
that a young person
who either marries or dies
is sure to be well spoken of.

—Jane Austen

The post-office has a great charm
at one period of our lives. When you have
lived to my age, you will begin
to think letters are never worth
going through the rain for.

—Jane Austen

The secret of staying young is to
live honestly, eat slowly,
and lie about your age.

—Lucille Ball

Happy Birthday

I am not half as patient with old women
now that I am one.

—Emily Carr

It is not all bad, this getting old, ripening.
After the fruit has got its growth
it should juice up and mellow. God forbid
I should live long enough to ferment
and rot and fall to the ground in a squash.

—Emily Carr

TWENTY CAN'T BE EXPECTED

to tolerate sixty

in all things, and sixty

gets bored stiff

with twenty's eternal love affairs.

—**Emily Carr**

Preparing for the worst
is an activity I have taken up
since I turned thirty-five,
and the worst actually began to happen.

—Delia Ephron

Maturity: A stoic response
to endless reality.

—Carrie Fisher

One of the many things
nobody ever tells you about middle age
is that it's such a nice change
from being young.

—Dorothy Canfield Fisher

This is a youth-oriented society,
and the joke is on them
because youth is a disease
from which we all recover.

—Dorothy Fuldheim

Quite a few women told me,
one way or another, that they thought
it was sex, not youth, that's wasted
on the young.

—Janet Harris

Don't let ol' folks tell you about
the good ol' days. I was there.
Where was they at?

—Jackie "Moms" Mabley

There ain't nothin' an ol' man
can do but bring me a message
from a young one.

—Jackie "Moms" Mabley

Old age is like a plane flying
through a storm. Once you're
aboard, there's nothing you can do.

—Golda Meir

Happy
Birthday

A woman, till five-and-thirty,

is only looked upon as a raw girl,

and can possibly make no noise in the world

till about forty. . . .

But 'tis a considerable comfort to me,

to know there is upon earth

such a paradise for old women.

—Lady Mary Wortley Montagu

I have always felt
that a woman has the right
to treat the subject of her age
with ambiguity until, perhaps,
she passes into the realm
of over ninety. Then it is better
she be candid with herself
and with the world.

—Helena Rubinstein

Time and trouble will tame
an advanced young woman, but an
advanced old woman is uncontrollable
by any earthly force.

—Dorothy Sayers

———

There are compensations for growing older.
One is the realization that to be sporting
isn't at all necessary. It is a great relief
to reach this stage of wisdom.

—Cornelia Otis Skinner

A girl can't analyze marriage,
and a woman—daren't.

—Lady Laura Troubridge

From birth to age eighteen,
a girl needs good parents.
From eighteen to thirty-five,
she needs good looks.
From thirty-five to fifty-five,
she needs a good personality.
From fifty-five on, she needs good cash.

—Sophie Tucker

Wisdom doesn't
automatically
come with old age.
Nothing does—except wrinkles.
It's true, some wines
improve with age. But only
if the grapes were good
in the first place.

—Abigail Van Buren

Religion and Morality

Principles are a dangerous form
of social dynamite.

—**Katharine Anthony**

A fool bolts pleasure,
then complains of moral indigestion.

—**Minna Antrim**

Women give themselves to God
when the devil wants nothing more
to do with them.

—Sophie Arnould

◄━━━━━━━━━━►

I'm the foe of moderation,
the champion of excess. . . . "I'd rather be
strongly wrong than weakly right."

—Tallulah Bankhead

Lead me not into temptation;
I can find the way myself.

—Rita Mae Brown

I had explained that a woman's asking
for equality in the church would be
comparable to a black person's
demanding equality in the Ku Klux Klan.

—Mary Daly

Our own theological Church,
as we know, has scorned
and vilified the body
till it has seemed
almost a reproach and a shame
to have one, yet at the same time
has credited it with power
to drag the soul to perdition.

—Eliza Farnham

You could say we've lost
our innocence.
That's a little worse
than losing the nickel
to put in Sunday school,
though not quite as bad
as losing the dime for
ice cream afterward.

—Nikki Giovanni

About Mary, mother of Jesus:

Because of her absolute purity and obedience, she is the only pinup girl who has been permitted in monks' cells throughout the ages.

—**Naomi Goldenberg**

THERE'S NOTHING IN THE WORLD

more ignorant

than to give any belief to ghosts.

I am walking the world

these twenty years

and I never met anything worse

than myself.

—**Lady Augusta Gregory**

Fashions in sin change.

—Lillian Hellman

I regard irreligious people
as pioneers. If there had been
no priesthood the world would have
advanced ten thousand times better
than it has now.

—Anandabai Joshee

There is nothing more innately human
than the tendency to transmute
what has become customary
into what has been divinely ordained.

—Suzanne LaFollette

God is love, but get it in writing.

—Gypsy Rose Lee

"God will protect us," [Mother] often said
to June and me. "But to make sure,"
she would add, "carry a heavy club."

—**Gypsy Rose Lee**

◆

Men who make no pretensions
to being good on one day out of seven
are called sinners.

—**Mary Wilson Little**

THE TOMBSTONE IS ABOUT

the only thing

that can stand upright

and lie on its face

at the same time.

—Mary Wilson Little

Sin has always been an ugly word,
but it has been made so
in a new sense over the last
half-century. It has been made
not only ugly but *passé*.
People are no longer sinful,
they are only immature or
underprivileged or frightened
or, more particularly, sick.

—**Phyllis McGinley**

Many are saved from sin
by being so inept at it.

—Mignon McLaughlin

There is a touch of optimism
in every worry about one's own
moral cleanliness.

—Victoria Ocampo

She was a good Christian woman
with a large respect for religion,
though she did not, of course,
believe any of it was true.

—Flannery O'Connor

———————◄

Discussing a job with a prospective employer:

Salary is no object; I want only enough
to keep body and soul apart.

—Dorothy Parker

The only thing that ever came back
from the grave that we know of
was a lie.

—Marilla Ricker

The Lord is not my shepherd.
I shall want.

—May Sarton

Of the worldly archbishop of Paris:

There are only two trifles
which make his
funeral ovation difficult—
the life and death
of the subject of it.

—**Marie de Sévigné**

If I had been the Virgin Mary,
I would have said "No."

—Stevie Smith

The Bible and Church have been
the greatest stumbling blocks
in the way of woman's emancipation.

—Elizabeth Cady Stanton

THE MEMORY OF MY OWN SUFFERING

has prevented me

from ever shadowing one young soul

with the superstitions

of the Christian religion.

—**Elizabeth Cady Stanton**

"You are so afraid
of losing your moral sense
that you are not willing
to take it through
anything more dangerous
than a mud-puddle."

—Gertrude Stein

I always find that statistics
are hard to swallow and
impossible to digest. The only one
I can ever remember is that
if all the people who go to sleep
in church were laid end to end
they would be
a lot more comfortable.

—Martha (Mrs. Robert A.) Taft

I was brought up
in a clergyman's household,
so I am a first-class liar.

—**Dame Sybil Thorndike**

"When we talk to God,
we're praying. When God talks to us,
we're schizophrenic."

—**Jane Wagner**

BETWEEN TWO EVILS,

I always pick the one

I never tried before.

—Mae West

I generally avoid temptation
unless I can't resist it.

—**Mae West**

What lies behind
the concept of decadence
to render it so appealing
to the imagination?

—**Renee Winegarten**

If you are open-minded,
things tend to fall out—
particularly those principles
and convictions by which
you define yourself.

—Sue Yarber

There is so little
basic difference between
total innocence
and complete degradation.

—Marguerite Yourcenar

The Arts

It's one of the tragic ironies of the theatre
that only one man in it can count on
steady work—the night watchman.

—Tallulah Bankhead

For an actress to be a success
she must have the face of Venus,
the brains of Minerva,
the grace of Terpsichore,
the memory of Macaulay, the figure of Juno,
and the hide of a rhinoceros.

—Ethel Barrymore

If Michelangelo were a heterosexual,
the Sistine Chapel would have been
painted basic white and with a roller.

—Rita Mae Brown

Theater people are always pining
and agonizing because they're afraid
that they'll be forgotten. And in America
they're quite right. They will be.

—Agnes de Mille

I mean, the question actors
most often get asked
is how they can bear saying
the same things over and over again
night after night, but God knows
the answer to that is,
don't we all anyway;
might as well get paid for it.

—Elaine Dundy

I have the conviction
that excessive literary production
is a social offense.

—George Eliot

THE CANNY AMONG THE PUBLISHERS

know that an enormous

popular appetite for the insulting

of the famous must be gratified,

and the modern biographer emerges

from the editorial conference

a sadist and a wiser man.

—Florence Kiper Frank

Some of the new books
are so down to earth
they ought to be ploughed under.

—Anne Herbert

The important thing in acting is to be able
to laugh and cry. If I have to cry,
I think of my sex life. If I have to laugh,
I think of my sex life.

—Glenda Jackson

The words "Kiss Kiss Bang Bang,"
which I saw on an Italian
movie poster, are perhaps
the briefest statement imaginable
of the basic appeal of movies.

—Pauline Kael

To write is to inform against others.

—**Violette Leduc**

Absurdly improbable things
happen in real life
as well as in weak literature.

—**Ada Leverson**

It was a book to kill time
for those who like it better dead.

—Rose Macaulay

Everywhere I go, I'm asked
if I think the universities stifle writers.
My opinion is that they don't stifle enough
of them. There's many a best seller
that could have been prevented
by a good teacher.

—Flannery O'Connor

In a book review:

This is not a novel to be tossed aside lightly. It should be thrown with great force.

—Dorothy Parker

The only "ism" Hollywood believes in
is plagiarism.

—Dorothy Parker

Actors cannot choose the manner
in which they are born. Consequently,
it is the one gesture in their lives
completely devoid
of self-consciousness.

—Helen Rowland

Television has lifted
the manufacture
of banality out of the sphere
of handicraft and placed it in that
of a major industry.

—Nathalie Sarraute

My only problem is finding a way
to play my fortieth fallen female
in a different way from my thirty-ninth.

—Barbara Stanwyck

Politics and Power

Stripped of ethical rationalizations
and philosophical pretensions,
a crime is anything that a group in power
chooses to prohibit.

—Freda Adler

To be loved is to be fortunate,
but to be hated is to achieve distinction.

—Minna Antrim

About David Lloyd George:

He could not see a belt
without hitting below it.

—Margot Asquith

After all, the eleventh commandment
(thou shalt not be found out)
is the only one that is virtually impossible
to keep in these days.

—Bertha Buxton

Under the philosophy
that now seems to guide our destinies,
nothing must get in the way of the man
with the spray gun.

—Rachel Carson

———————————

I shall be an autocrat; that's my trade.
And the good Lord will forgive me; that's His.

—Catherine II, Empress of Russia

Oh, say not foreign war!
A war is never foreign.

—Marie von Ebner-Eschenbach

No politics remains innocent of
that which it contests.

—Elizabeth Fox-Genovese

I've been married to one Marxist
and one Fascist, and neither one
would take the garbage out.

—Lee Grant

Progress everywhere today
does seem to come so very heavily
disguised as Chaos.

—Joyce Grenfell

Going crazy has always been
a personal solution in extremis
to the unarticulated conflicts
of political realities.

—Jill Johnston

I had the correct instinct to fuck things up
but no political philosophy to clarify
a course of action.

—Jill Johnston

It is interesting to speculate
how it developed that
in two of the most
anti-feminist institutions,
the church
and the law court,
the men
are wearing the dresses.

—Florynce Kennedy

What you Kansas farmers ought to do
is to raise less corn and raise more hell.

—**Mary Lease**

No influence so quickly converts
a radical into a reactionary
as does his election to power.

—**Elisabeth Marbury**

In politics, it seems,
retreat is honorable
if dictated by military considerations
and shameful if even *suggested*
for ethical reasons.

—**Mary McCarthy**

I am become a socialist.
I love humanity; but I hate people.

—**Edna St. Vincent Millay**

"WHAT MOST PEOPLE DON'T SEEM

to realize

is that there is just as much

money to be made

out of the wreckage of a civilization

as from the upbuilding of one."

—Margaret Mitchell

The usefulness of madmen is famous;
they demonstrate society's logic flagrantly
carried out down to its last scrimshaw scrap.

—**Cynthia Ozick**

Profits and prostitution—upon these empires
are built and kingdoms stand.

—**Adela Pankhurst**

The mistake a lot of politicians make
is in forgetting they've been appointed
and thinking they've been anointed.

—Mildred (Mrs. Claude) Pepper

What moron said that knowledge is power?
Knowledge is power only if it doesn't
depress you so much that it leaves you
in an immobile heap at the end
of your bed.

—Paula Poundstone

Nothing is as difficult
as to achieve results
in this world
if one is filled full
of great tolerance
and the milk
of human kindness.

—**Corinne Roosevelt Robinson**

The single most impressive fact
about the attempt by American women
to obtain the right to vote is
how long it took.

—Alice Rossi

The best way to win an argument
is to begin by being right.

—Jill Ruckelshaus

The prohibition law,
written for weaklings
and derelicts, has divided
the nation, like Gaul,
into three parts—
wets, drys and hypocrites.

—**Florence Sabin**

Life in this society being, at best,
an utter bore and no aspect of society being
at all relevant to women, there remains
to civic-minded, responsible,
thrill-seeking females only to overthrow
the government, eliminate the money system,
institute complete automation
and destroy the male sex.

—Valerie Solanis

Reformers, who are always compromising,
have not yet grasped the idea that truth
is the only safe ground to stand on.

—Elizabeth Cady Stanton

Thousands of dollars are wasted every year
over unsightly statues. If these great men
must have outdoor memorials
let them be in the form of handsome blocks
of buildings for the poor.

—Elizabeth Cady Stanton

In politics,
if you want anything said,
ask a man;
if you want anything done,
ask a woman.

—Margaret Thatcher

The older you get the more you realize
that gray isn't such a bad color.
And in politics you work with it
or you don't work at all.

—Agnes Sligh Turnbull

People who fight fire with fire
usually end up with ashes.

—Abigail Van Buren

"The trouble with the rat race is that even if you win, you're still a rat."

—**Jane Wagner**

"Years ago, fairy tales all began with "Once upon a time . . ." —now we know they all begin with "If I am elected."

—**Carolyn Warner**

When I am sick, then I believe in law.

—**Anna Wickham**

Unequal Rights

Housewife: One who is
more married to a house
than to the man she once thought
it was all about.

—Anonymous

If any histories were anciently written
by women, time and the malice of men
have effectually conspir'd to suppress 'em.

—Mary Astell

If I had been born a man, I would have
conquered Europe. As I was born a woman,
I exhausted my energies in tirades
against fate, and in eccentricities.

—Maria Konstantinovna Bashkirtseff

I don't drink or do any drugs. I never have
and I never will. I don't need them.
I'm a Black woman from the land of the free,
home of the brave and I figure
I don't need another illusion.

—Bertice Berry

Men are not opposed to women working,
just against their being paid for it.

—Barbara Bodichon

For such despite they cast on Female wits:
If what I do prove well, it won't advance,
They'll say it's stolen, or else it was by chance.

—Anne Bradstreet

When I ran for D.C. City Council
one of the reporters who interviewed me
mentioned that my problem was that
I was always considered to be on the Left.
I said, "Well, I know that people have said
I was left, and I agreed with them that yeah,
I had been left out and left behind
and left over."

—Josephine Butler

Life as a child and then as a girl
had taught her patience, hope, silence;
and given her a prisoner's proficiency
in handling these virtues as weapons.

—Colette

I am working for the time when
unqualified blacks, browns and women
join the unqualified men in running
our government.

—Frances T. "Cissy" Farenthold

Well, I'm convinced that many frustrated
and crabby women are merely
feminists in restraints.

—Diane F. Germain

Boys and girls are expected, also,
to behave differently to each other,
and to people in general—a behavior
to be briefly described in two words.
To the boy we say, "Do"; to the girl, "Don't."

—Charlotte Perkins Gilman

There is no female mind.
The brain is not an organ of sex.
As well speak of a female liver.

—Charlotte Perkins Gilman

It is an immense loss
to have all robust and sustaining expletives
refined away from one!
At . . . moments of trial, refinement
is a feeble reed to lean upon.

—Alice James

We haven't come a long way,
we've come a short way.
If we hadn't come a short way,
no one would be calling us "baby."

—Elizabeth Janeway

Gossip is the opiate
of the oppressed.

—Erica Jong

CUCKOLD: THE HUSBAND of an unfaithful wife.

The wife of an unfaithful husband

is just called *wife*.

—Cheris Kramarae and Paula Treichler

Most people, no doubt,
when they espouse human rights,
make their own mental reservations
about the proper application
of the word "human."

—Suzanne LaFollette

Powerful men often succeed
through the help of their wives.
Powerful women only succeed
in spite of their husbands.

—Linda Lee-Potter

College for women was a refinement
whose main purpose was to better
prepare you for your ultimate destiny . . .
to make you a more desirable product.

—Pat Loud

The sum and substance
of female education in America, as in England,
is training women to consider marriage
as the sole object in life, and to pretend
that they do not think so.

—Harriet Martineau

If women may not work in mines,
why should men be allowed
to paint teacups?

—Lady Laura McLaren

———————

"I have no wish for a second husband.
I had enough of the first.
I like to have my own way—
to lie down mistress, and get up master."

—Susanna Moodie

No *man,* not even a doctor,
ever gives any other definition
of what a nurse should be—
"devoted and obedient."
This definition would do just as well
for a porter. It might even do
for a horse. It would not do
for a policeman.

—Florence Nightingale

I do not ask for my rights.
I have no rights; I have only wrongs.

—Caroline Norton

To the old saying that man built the house
but woman made of it a "home"
might be added the modern supplement
that woman accepted cooking
as a chore but man has made of it
a recreation.

—Emily Post

Why should we mind
if men have their faces on the money,
as long as we get our hands on it?

—Ivy Baker Priest

Give women scope and opportunity,
and they will be no worse than men.

—Nelly Ptaschkina

"No chivalry prevents men
from getting women
at the very lowest possible wage."

—Elizabeth Robins

Woman: the peg on which
the wit hangs his jest, the preacher
his text, the cynic his grouch,
and the sinner his justification.

—Helen Rowland

"If the bird *does* like its cage,
and *does* like its sugar, and will not leave it,
why keep the door so very carefully shut?"

—Olive Schreiner

"It is delightful to be a woman;
but every man thanks the Lord devoutly
that he isn't one."

—Olive Schreiner

THEY ARE CALLED FINISHING-SCHOOLS

and the name tells accurately

what they are.

They finish everything.

—Olive Schreiner

Legislation and case law still exist
in some parts of the United States
permitting the "passion shooting"
by a husband of a wife; the reverse,
of course, is known as homicide.

—Diane B. Schulder

Well, banality is a terribly likely consequence
of the underuse of a good mind.
That is why in particular it is
a female affliction.

—Cynthia Propper Seton

Why was everything nice
he did for me a bribe or a favor,
while my kindnesses to him were my duty?

—Alix Kates Shulman

I have always felt that one great advantage
of being both Black and a woman
was that I started off with
nothing to lose.

—Naomi Sims

A successful woman preacher was once
asked "what special obstacles have you met
as a woman in the ministry?" "Not one,"
she answered, "except the lack
of a minister's wife."

—Anna Garlin Spencer

And when her biographer says of an
Italian woman poet, "during some years
her Muse was intermitted," we do not wonder
at the fact when he casually mentions
her ten children.

—Anna Garlin Spencer

I am at a boiling point! If I do not find some day the use of my tongue on this question I shall die of an intellectual repression, a woman's rights convulsion.

—**Elizabeth Cady Stanton**

I have come to the conclusion that the first great work to be accomplished for women is to revolutionize the dogma that sex is a crime, marriage a defilement, and maternity a bane.

—**Elizabeth Cady Stanton**

I think if women would indulge
more freely in vituperation, they would
enjoy ten times the health they do.
It seems to me they are suffering
from repression.

—Elizabeth Cady Stanton

The more complete the despotism,
the more smoothly all things move
on the surface.

—Elizabeth Cady Stanton

Woman's discontent increases
in exact proportion to her development.

—**Elizabeth Cady Stanton**

◄——————————►

The great and almost only comfort
about being a woman is that one can always
pretend to be more stupid than one is
and no one is surprised.

—**Freya Stark**

For a woman to get a rewarding
sense of total creation by way of
the multiple monotonous chores
that are her daily lot
would be as irrational as
for an assembly line worker
to rejoice that he had created
an automobile because
he tightened a bolt.

—**Edith Mendel Stern**

The role of the housewife
is, therefore, analogous to that
of the president of a corporation
who would not only determine
policies and make over-all plans
but also spend the major part
of his time and energy
in such activities as sweeping
the plant and oiling the machines.

—**Edith Mendel Stern**

About British legal documents of the nineteenth century:

The word *man*
always includes *woman*
when there is a penalty
to be incurred, it never includes
women when there is a privilege
to be conferred.

—**Charlotte Carmichael Stopes**

How . . . comes it to passe, that when
a Father hath a numerous issue of Sonnes
and Daughters, the sonnes forsooth are . . .
trained up in the Liberall Arts and Sciences,
and there [if they prove not Block-heads]
they may in time be book-learned while . . .
we . . . are set onely to the Needle,
to pricke our fingers: or else to the Wheele
to spinne a faire thread for our
owne undoings.

—"Mary Tattlewell" and "Joan Hit-him-home"

If the first woman God ever made
was strong enough to turn the world
upside down all alone, these women together
ought to be able to turn it back,
and get it right side up again!

—Sojourner Truth

But oh, what a woman I should be
if an able young man would consecrate
his life to me as secretaries and technicians do
to their men employers.

—Mabel Ulrich

Women have to make jokes
about themselves, laugh about themselves,
because they have nothing to lose.

—**Agnes Varda**

If I had been a man, self-respect,
family pressure and the public opinion
of my class would have pushed me
into a money-making profession;
as a mere woman I could carve out a career
of disinterested research.

—**Beatrice Potter Webb**

What we had to do was . . .
to make medical treatment
not a favour granted
to those in desperate need
but to compel all sick persons
to submit to it . . . to treat illness,
in fact, as a public nuisance
to be suppressed in the interests
of the community.

—Beatrice Potter Webb

I myself have never been able to find out precisely what feminism is: I only know that people call me a feminist whenever I express sentiments that differentiate me from a doormat or a prostitute.

—Rebecca West

Whatever women do they must do twice as well as men to be thought half as good. Luckily, this is not difficult.

—Charlotte Whitton

The *divine right* of husbands, like the divine right of kings, may, it is hoped, in this enlightened age, be contested without danger.

—**Mary Wollstonecraft**

———◄———

Women have served all these centuries as looking-glasses possessing the magic and delicious power of reflecting the figure of man at twice its natural size.

—**Virginia Woolf**

THE RIGHT EDUCATION

of the Female Sex,

as it is in a manner everywhere neglected,

so it ought to be generally lamented.

Most in this depraved later Age Think

a Woman learned and wise enough

if she can distinguish her Husbands Bed

from anothers.

—Hannah Woolley

Hard Currency

The poor man's motto,
"Women's work is never done,"
leads inevitably to its antithesis—
ladies' work is never begun.

—Antoinette Blackwell

◄————————►

We owe something to extravagance,
for thrift and adventure seldom go
hand in hand.

—Jenny Churchill

To be satisfied with little is hard,
to be satisfied with a lot, impossible.

—Marie von Ebner-Eschenbach

Providing for one's family
as a good husband and father
is a water-tight excuse
for making money hand over fist.

—Eva Figes

Now that he was rich
he was not thought ignorant any more,
but simply eccentric.

—Mavis Gallant

The women who do the most work
get the least money, and the women
who have the most money
do the least work.

—Charlotte Perkins Gilman

What I know about money,
I learned the hard way—by having had it.

—Margaret Halsey

———◆———

No one has yet had the courage
to memorialize his wealth on his tombstone.
A dollar mark would not look well there.

—Corra May Harris

Men always try to keep women
out of business so they won't find out
how much fun it really is.

—**Vivian Kellems**

"You don't seem to realize that
a poor person who is unhappy
is in a better position than a rich person
who is unhappy. Because the poor person
has hope. He thinks money would help."

—**Jean Kerr**

IF I WERE HONEST,

I would admit

that money is one half of happiness;

it makes it so much more attractive.

—**Marie Lenéru**

Money is only money,
beans tonight and steak tomorrow.
So long as you can look yourself
in the eye.

—**Meridel Le Sueur**

The richer your friends,
the more they will cost you.

—**Elisabeth Marbury**

We have a little catch phrase
in our family which somehow
fits almost everyone in the movie colony:
"Spare no expense to make everything
as economical as possible."

—Frances Marion

When an American heiress
wants to buy a man,
she at once crosses the Atlantic.

—Mary McCarthy

It's only the rich
in their guilt and denial
who can really afford
to be downwardly mobile.

—"Morena"

A LADY, THAT IS AN ENLIGHTENED,

cultivated, liberal lady—

the only kind to be in a time of

increasing classlessness—could espouse

any cause: wayward girls, social diseases,

unmarried mothers, and/or birth control

with impunity. But never by so much as

the shadow of a look should she acknowledge

her own experience with the Facts of Life.

—Virgilia Peterson

228

In modern society as in ancient cultures,
noticing who schleps and carries
tells us a lot about who is usually left
holding the bag.

—Letty Cottin Pogrebin

Until changing economic conditions
made the thing actually happen,
struggling early society would hardly
have guessed that woman's road to gentility
would lie through doing nothing at all.

—Emily James Putnam

A fool and her money
are soon counted.

—Helen Rowland

Although there are countless
alumni of the school of hard knocks,
there has not yet been a move
to accredit that institution.

—Sonya Rudikoff

The keeping of an idle woman
is a badge of superior social status.

—**Dorothy L. Sayers**

While I am hardly advocating
"Service with a Snarl," I find myself
occasionally wishing for
"Service with a Deadpan," or just plain
Service, executed with efficiency
and minus all the Charm School garnish.

—**Cornelia Otis Skinner**

I do want to get rich,
but I never want to do
what there is to do to get rich.

—Gertrude Stein

No one would have remembered
the Good Samaritan if he'd
only had good intentions.
He had money as well.

—Margaret Thatcher

Pennies do not come from heaven.
They have to be earned here on earth.

—Margaret Thatcher

───◆───

Some people are more turned on
by money than they are by love. . . .
In one respect they're alike.
They're both wonderful
as long as they last.

—Abigail Van Buren

"THEN WHY DON'T ALL GIRLS

belong to unions?"

I asked, feeling very much an outsider;

but she of the gents' neckwear replied:

"Well, there's some that thinks

it ain't fashionable; there's some that thinks

it ain't no use; and there's some

that never thinks at all."

—Maud Younger

Social Encounters

To know oneself is wisdom,
but to know one's neighbor is genius.

—Minna Antrim

Who can begin conventional amiability
the first thing in the morning? It is the hour
of savage instincts and natural tendencies;
it is the triumph of the Disagreeable
and the Cross. I am convinced that
the Muses and the Graces never thought of
having breakfast anywhere but in bed.

—Countess von Arnim

I do not want people to be very agreeable,
as it saves me the trouble
of liking them a great deal.

—Jane Austen

The idea of strictly minding
our own business is moldy rubbish.
Who could be so selfish?

—Myrtie Lillian Barker

He that will live in this world
must be endued with
the three rare qualities
of dissimulation, equivocation,
and mental reservation.

—Aphra Behn

People would have more leisure time
if it weren't for all the leisure-time activities
that use it up.

—Peg Bracken

Whenever anyone tells me that he or she
has a headache, has business letters
to write,—doesn't want to be disturbed,—
I take it for granted that he or she is engaged
in something nothing less than wicked—
and naturally I don't want to know
anything about it!

—Harriet L. Childe-Pemberton

My true friends have always given me
that supreme proof of devotion,
a spontaneous aversion for the man I love.

—Colette

Blessed is the man who,
having nothing to say,
abstains from giving in words evidence
of the fact.

—George Eliot

AMONG THE MOST DISHEARTENING
and dangerous of . . .
advisors, you will often find those closest
to you, your dearest friends, members of
your own family, perhaps, loving,
anxious, and knowing nothing whatever.

—Minnie Fiske

Most people hew the battlements
of life from compromise,
erecting their impregnable keeps
from judicious submissions,
fabricating their philosophical
drawbridges from emotional
retractions and scalding marauders
in the boiling oil of sour grapes.

—Zelda Fitzgerald

I'll not listen to reason. . . . Reason always means what someone else has got to say.

—**Elizabeth Gaskell**

They did not know the pathology of epigram, the basic truth of which is that word-intoxicated people express an opinion long before they dream of holding it.

—**Katharine Gerould**

A family unity which is only
bound together with a table-cloth
is of questionable value.

—Charlotte Perkins Gilman

In society it is etiquette for ladies
to have the best chairs and get handed things.
In the home the reverse is the case.
That is why ladies are more sociable
than gentlemen.

—Virginia Graham

I have often relied on the
blindness of strangers.

—Adrienne E. Gusoff

Such leaping to foot, such opening of doors,
such lightning flourishes with matches
and cigarettes—it is all so heroic,
I never quite get over the feeling
that someone has just said,
"To the lifeboats!"

—Margaret Halsey

Next to entertaining or impressive talk,
a thoroughgoing silence manages to intrigue
most people.

—Florence Hurst Harriman

Cynicism is an unpleasant way
of saying the truth.

—Lillian Hellman

Trying to be fascinating
is an asinine position to be in.

—Katharine Hepburn

There cannot be found in the animal kingdom
a bat, or any other creature, so blind in its
own range of circumstance and connection,
as the greater majority of human beings
are in the bosoms of their families.

—Helen Hunt Jackson

It has long been my belief that in times
of great stress, such as a four-day vacation,
the thin veneer of family unity wears off
almost at once, and we are revealed
in our true personalities.

—Shirley Jackson

Dorothy, like a good many
bad-tempered people, was quick
to forgive affronts, so that she could start
giving and receiving them again.

—**Pamela Hansford Johnson**

"Even though a number of people
have tried, no one has yet found a way
to drink for a living."

—**Jean Kerr**

Television has proved
that people will look at anything
rather than each other.

—**Ann Landers**

Large, naked, raw carrots
are acceptable as food
only to those who live in hutches
eagerly awaiting Easter.

—**Fran Lebowitz**

The opposite of talking isn't listening.
The opposite of talking is waiting.

—Fran Lebowitz

The telephone is a good way to talk to people
without having to offer them a drink.

—Fran Lebowitz

If you haven't got anything nice to say
about anybody, come sit next to me.

—Alice Roosevelt Longworth

LYING INCREASES THE CREATIVE
faculties, expands the ego, lessens
the friction of social contacts . . . it is only
in lies, wholeheartedly and bravely told,
that human nature attains through words
and speech the forbearance, the nobility,
the romance, the idealism, that—
being what it is—it falls so short of
in fact and in deed.

—Clare Boothe Luce

He talked and talked
because he didn't know what to say.

—Dacia Maraini

The dying process begins
the minute we are born, but it accelerates
during dinner parties.

—Carol Matthau

Brains are always awkward at a gay
and festive party.

—Elsa Maxwell

He had never outgrown
the feeling that a quest for
information was a series of
maneuvers in a game of espionage.

—Mary McCarthy

Moral: In saying what is obvious,
never choose cunning.
Yelling works better.

—Cynthia Ozick

When Dogs fall on snarling,
Serpents on hissing, and Women on weeping,
the first meanes to bite, the second to sting,
and the last to deceive.

—"R.M."

We were young enough still
to harbor the glad illusion
that organized forms of get-together
were commendable.

—Cornelia Otis Skinner

No man is responsible for his father.
That is entirely his mother's affair.

—Margaret Turnbull

Celebrities used to be found in clusters,
like oysters—and with much the same
efensive mechanisms.

—Barbara Walters

Incessant company is as bad
as solitary confinement.

—Virginia Woolf

Places and Peoples

English men are like that.
They love life more and value it less
than any other people in the world.

—Zöe Akins

What a pity,
when Christopher Columbus
discovered America,
that he ever mentioned it.

—Margot Asquith

The English have always been
a wicked race. . . . It has been noticed that
islanders are always more treacherous
and wicked than the inhabitants of terra firma.

—Charlotte Elizabeth of Bavaria

Murdering the King's English
can be a crime only if you identify
with the King.

—Judy Grahn

American interiors tend to have
no happy medium between execrable taste
and what is called "good taste"
and is worn like a wart.

—**Margaret Halsey**

In England, having had money . . .
is just as acceptable as having it. . . .
But never having had money is unforgivable,
and can only be atoned for
by never trying to get any.

—**Margaret Halsey**

It takes a great deal to produce
ennui in an Englishman and if you do,
he only takes it as convincing proof
that you are well bred.

—**Margaret Halsey**

The English never smash in a face.
They merely refrain
from asking it to dinner.

—**Margaret Halsey**

The English think of an opinion
as something which a decent person,
if he has the misfortune to have one,
does all he can to hide.

—**Margaret Halsey**

There is not enough loving-kindness afloat
in the continental United States
to see a crippled old lady
across an Indian trail.

—**Margaret Halsey**

Years ago I heard somebody say that being a Roumanian was not a nationality, but a profession.

—**Lillian Hellman**

A Scotchman said that he did not leave his country for *want*; he had enough of that there.

—**Lady Holland**

In some parts of Ireland the sleep
which knows no waking
is always followed by a wake
which knows no sleeping.

—Mary Wilson Little

Europeans used to say Americans
were puritanical. Then they discovered
that we were not puritans. So now they say
we are obsessed with sex.

—Mary McCarthy

When I'm asked why Southern writers particularly have a penchant for writing about freaks, I say it's because we are still able to recognize one.

—Flannery O'Connor

I was born in Alabama, but I only lived there for a month before I'd done everything there was to do.

—Paula Poundstone

Philadelphians are every whit
as mediocre as their neighbours, but they
seldom encourage each other in mediocrity
by giving it a more agreeable name.

—Agnes Repplier

The trouble with most Englishwomen
is that they *will* dress as if they had been
a mouse in a previous incarnation.

—Edith Sitwell

In the United States there is more space
where nobody is than where anybody is.
That is what makes America what it is.

—**Gertrude Stein**

More great Americans were failures
than they were successes. They mostly spent
their lives in not having a buyer
for what they had for sale.

—**Gertrude Stein**

Native always means people who belong somewhere else, because they had once belonged somewhere. That shows that the white race does not really think they belong anywhere because they think of everybody else as native.

—**Gertrude Stein**

The Jews have produced only three originative geniuses: Christ, Spinoza, and myself.

—**Gertrude Stein**

I moved to New York City for my health.
I'm paranoid and it was the only place
where my fears were justified.

—Anita Weiss

Those comfortably padded lunatic asylums
which are known, euphemistically,
as the stately homes of England.

—Virginia Woolf

Men

Man forgives woman anything
save the wit to outwit him.

—Minna Antrim

———————

In passing, also, I would like to say that
the first time Adam had a chance
he laid the blame on woman.

—Nancy Astor

No man needs curing of his individual sickness; his universal malady is what he should look to.

—Djuna Barnes

Any survey of what businessmen are reading runs smack into the open secret that most businessmen aren't. Reading books, that is.

—Marilyn Bender

My ancestors wandered lost
in the wilderness for forty years
because even in biblical times,
men would not stop to ask for directions.

—Elayne Boosler

When women are depressed
they either eat or go shopping.
Men invade another country.
It's a whole different way of thinking.

—Elayne Boosler

Men get opinions as boys learn to spell,
by reiteration chiefly.

—Elizabeth Barrett Browning

———————

To a man:
Do you know why God withheld
the sense of humour from women?
That we may love you
instead of laughing at you.

—Beatrice (Mrs. Patrick) Campbell

An intelligent woman has millions of born enemies . . . all the stupid men.

—Marie von Ebner-Eschenbach

I'm not denyin' the women are foolish; God almighty made 'em to match the men."

—George Eliot

If men can run the world,
why can't they stop wearing neckties?
How intelligent is it to start the day
by tying a little noose around your neck?

—Linda Ellerbee

A man in love is incomplete
until he has married.
Then he's finished.

—Zsa Zsa Gabor

Seems nothing draws men together like killing other men.

—Susan Glaspell

A man's home may seem to be his castle on the outside; inside, it is more often his nursery.

—Clare Boothe Luce

When a man can't explain a woman's actions,
the first thing he thinks about is
the condition of her uterus.

—Clare Boothe Luce

Women want mediocre men, and men
are working hard to be as mediocre as possible.

—Margaret Mead

Don't accept rides from strange men,
and remember that all men are strange as hell.

—Robin Morgan

Men will always opt for things
that get finished and stay that way—
putting up screens, but not
planning menus.

—Jane O'Reilly

I require only three things
of a man. He must be handsome,
ruthless and stupid.

—Dorothy Parker

The difference between
government bonds and men
is that government bonds mature.

—Debby Perry

An emotional man may possess no humor,
but a humorous man usually has
deep pockets of emotion,
sometimes tucked away or forgotten.

—Constance Rourke

A bachelor never quite gets over the idea
that he is a thing of beauty
and a boy forever.

—Helen Rowland

It takes a woman twenty years
to make a man of her son,
and another woman twenty minutes
to make a fool of him.

—Helen Rowland

Never trust a husband too far,
nor a bachelor too near.

—Helen Rowland

Give a man a fish and he eats for a day.
Teach him how to fish
and you get rid of him for the whole weekend.

—Zenna Schaffer

I fear nothing so much
as a man who is witty all day long.

—Marie de Sévigné

Though woman needs the protection
of one man against his whole sex . . .
she sometimes needs, too, the protection
of all men against this one.

—**Elizabeth Cady Stanton**

Wherever the skilled hands and cultured brain
of women have made the battle of life easier
for man, he has readily pardoned her sound
judgment and proper self-assertion.

—**Elizabeth Cady Stanton**

IT IS FUNNY THE TWO THINGS

most men are proudest of

is the thing that any man can do

and doing does in the same way,

that is being drunk

and being the father of their son.

—Gertrude Stein

A man, it seems, may be intellectually
in complete sympathy with a woman's aims.
But only about ten percent of him
is his intellect—the other ninety his emotions.

—Mabel Ulrich

*In response to a man who said, "Much of this talk
about feminism is nonsense: Any woman would rather be
beautiful than clever":*

Quite true. But that is because so many men
are stupid and so few are blind.

—Beatrice Potter Webb

I blame Rousseau, myself. "Man is born free,"
indeed. Man is not born free,
he is born attached to his mother
by a cord and is not capable of looking after
himself for at least seven years
(seventy in some cases).

—Katharine Whitehorn

The only time a woman really succeeds
in changing a man is when he's a baby.

—Natalie Wood

Being Human

I am one of those people
who just can't help getting a kick out of life—
even when it's a kick in the teeth.

—Polly Adler

I didn't know what to do about life—
so I did a nervous breakdown
that lasted many months.

—Margaret Anderson

My unreality is chiefly this:
I have never felt much like a human being.
It's a splendid feeling.

—**Margaret Anderson**

A woman, especially if she have
the misfortune of knowing anything,
should conceal it as well as she can.

—**Jane Austen**

If I had to live my life again I'd make
all the same mistakes—only sooner.

—Tallulah Bankhead

Just being in a room with myself
is almost more stimulation than I can bear.

—Kate Braverman

Reputation is a bubble which a man bursts
when he tries to blow it for himself.

—Emma Carleton

I am no longer what I was.
I will remain what I have become.

—**Coco Chanel**

There goes a woman who knows
all the things that can be taught
and none of the things that
cannot be taught.

—**Coco Chanel**

Many a person professes
to have a good heart, but in truth
has only weak nerves.

—Marie von Ebner-Eschenbach

Millions long for immortality
who do not know what to do
with themselves
on a rainy Sunday afternoon.

—Susan Ertz

There is no point at which you can say,
"Well, I'm successful now. I might as well
take a nap."

—Carrie Fisher

If women can sleep their way to the top,
how come they aren't there? . . .
There must be an epidemic
of insomnia out there.

—Ellen Goodman

NEVER GIVE UP. . . .

A little money helps,

but what *really* gets it right is to *never*—

I repeat—*never* under any conditions

face the facts.

—Ruth Gordon

Humility is not my forte, and whenever I dwell for any length of time on my own shortcomings, they gradually begin to seem mild, harmless, rather engaging little things, not at all like the staring defects in other people's characters.

—**Margaret Halsey**

I don't care what is written about me
so long as it isn't true.

—**Katharine Hepburn**

And so it criticized each flower,
This supercilious seed;
Until it woke one summer hour,
And found itself a weed.

—**Mildred Howells**

How sick one gets of being "good,"
how much I should respect myself
if I could burst out and make every one
wretched for twenty-four hours;
embody selfishness.

—Alice James

I suppose one has a greater sense
of intellectual degradation after an interview
with a doctor than from any
human experience.

—Alice James

I feel about airplanes
the way I feel about diets.
It seems to me that they are wonderful things
for other people to go on.

—Jean Kerr

Success is something I will dress for
when I get there, and not until.
Cross my heart and hope to die.

—Fran Lebowitz

Books, books, these are the only things
that have come to my aid! In the end,
it makes one terribly arrogant always to do
without one's equals.

—Marie Lenéru

◄————————►

The first rule in opera is the first rule in life:
see to everything yourself.

—Nellie Melba

"Until you've lost your reputation, you never realize what a burden it was or what freedom really is."

—Margaret Mitchell

The affair between Margot Asquith and Margot Asquith will live as one of the prettiest love stories in all literature.

—Dorothy Parker

I totally and completely admit,
with no qualms at all, my egomania,
my selfishness, coupled with
a really magnificent voice.

—Leontyne Price

A woman is like a teabag—
you can't tell how strong she is
until you put her in hot water.

—Nancy Reagan

If you think you're too small to have
an impact, try going to bed with a mosquito.

—Anita Roddick

I am so glad I never *feel* important,
it does complicate life.

—Eleanor Roosevelt

No one can make you feel inferior
without your consent.

—Eleanor Roosevelt

I had never been as resigned
to ready-made ideas as I was
to ready-made clothes, perhaps because,
although I couldn't sew, I could think.

—Jane Rule

I have seen some souls so compressed
that they would have fitted
into a small thimble, and found room
to move there—wide room.

—Olive Schreiner

If it is true
that we have sprung
from the ape,
there are occasions
when my own spring
appears not to have been
very far.

—Cornelia Otis Skinner

It requires philosophy and heroism
to rise above the opinion of the wise men
of all nations and races.

—**Elizabeth Cady Stanton**

Womanhood is the great fact
in her life;
wifehood and motherhood
are but incidental relations.

—**Elizabeth Cady Stanton**

I could undertake
to be an efficient pupil
if it were possible
to find an efficient teacher.

—Gertrude Stein

It takes a lot of time to be a genius,
you have to sit around so much
doing nothing, really doing nothing.

—Gertrude Stein

ONE NEVER DISCUSSES ANYTHING

with anybody

who can understand

one discusses things

with people

who cannot understand.

—Gertrude Stein

Self-esteem isn't everything;
it's just that there's nothing without it.

—Gloria Steinem

Self-confidence: When you think
that your greatest fault
is being too hard on yourself.

—Judith Viorst

"Delusions of grandeur
make me feel a lot better
about myself."

—Jane Wagner

Author
Index